MEET THE DOSHAS

YOGA PHILOSOPHY FOR YOUNG HEARTS
BOOK 2

STORY AND PICTURES BY
STEFANIE "YOGA BUNNY" JILLIAN

Meet the Doshas
Yoga Philosophy for Young Hearts
Series Book 2

©2019 Stefanie Jillian
Avigna Health & Wellness
Integrative Education

ISBN 978-0-9990159-0-2
Library of Congress 2017918245

Printed in the United States of America
First Printing 2019

Written and Illustrated by Stefanie Jillian

www.AvignaHealth.com

"The meaning of Karma is in the intention. The intention behind action is what matters. Those who are motivated only by desire for the fruits of action are miserable, for they are constantly anxious about the results of what they do."

- The Bhagavad Gita

This book is dedicated to your inner "baby nut-ball"- the part of yourself that wants to welcome in a little more balance and calm. And to my baby nut-balls, Truss and Ember.

May you find peace, unconditional love, and contentment.

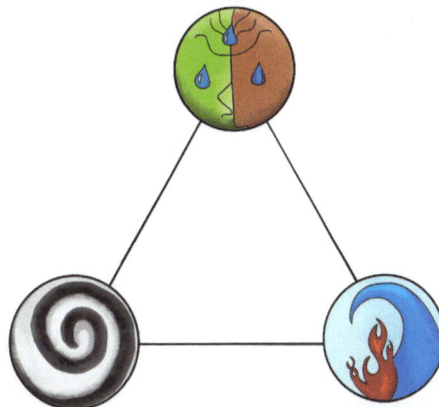

Sanskrit Pronunciation

Dosha   : doe-sha

Akasha   : ah-ka-sha

Vayu   : vie-you

Agni   : ah-g-nee

Jala   : ja-la

Prithvi   : prih-th-vee

Vata   : vah-tah

Pitta   : pih- ta

Kapha   : kah- fah

Prakruti : prah-krew-tee

Vikruti   : vih-krew-tee

These three best friends are as close as can be. Together they are called the Doshas. Meet Vata, Pitta, and Kapha.

Pitta and Kapha are not only best friends, they are also half-sisters!

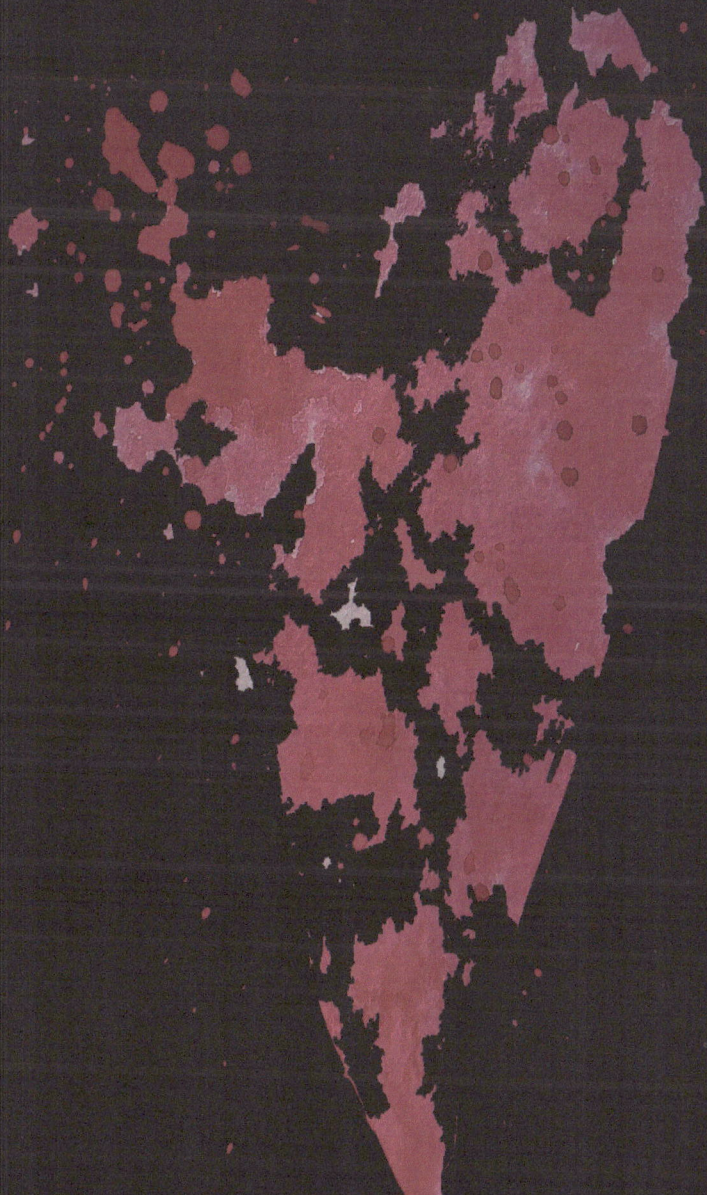

First...
Let's learn a little more about who the Doshas' parents are.

The Five Great Elements are the foundation for all of life. Akasha, Vayu, Agni, Jala and Prithvi come together to form all life here on our planet.

Akasha is the space between the molecules of us all, she is the endless ether that spans the universe.

Vayu is the air that moves, and senses delicate vibrations.

Akasha and Vayu, or space and air, are the parents of Vata.

7

Agni is the fire that burns, the heat that births action.

Jala is the water that flows through all, giving life.

Agni and Jala, fire and water, are the parents of Pitta.

Jala could not be contained and he rushed away like flood water down into a valley and basked in the beauty he saw in the tree topped mountains that grew out of the earth.

11

Prithvi is the earth body, the food that grows, and the mountain top homes.

Prithvi and Jala are the parents of Kapha. She was born near the edge of the ocean, out of water and earth.

The Doshas are very close friends, like a sisterhood. But they are each very different.

Vata was born in the fall and loves the cold, dry air. She is often restless and moves fast like the wind. Vata is creative and smart but sometimes forgets and leaves projects unfinished. She has a hard time relaxing because she is always very busy, and gets tired easily.

Vata has learned that if she takes the time to sit down she will feel better. She closes her eyes and thinks about the space and air around and inside her body, starting at the top of her head. She thinks about her entire body ending at the feet and other parts of her that are on the ground. Vata needs to sit on the earth to calm her when she seems to be swirling like a tornado. This is called Meditation.

16

Her friend, Pitta, was born in the summer. She dances and flows with the balance of fire and water. Pitta has a big heart full of love but sometimes can get angry and hot like fire.

Pitta needs to cool down and practices yoga poses that line up in a certain way. She then sits and thinks about the earth underneath her and her entire body, moving up to her heart, where she thinks about how she can be selfless and caring towards others. Pitta also likes to take long walks where she will think about nothing, or everything, or something in between.

Pitta is passionate and gets things done!
Often her friend Vata will have a creative idea and will ask Pitta to
help her complete the mission.

19

One day, Vata had the idea to raise money to pay for yoga classes for people that didn't have the money to go.

But as you know, Vata can tend to swirl around having so many good ideas at once, that she can't seem to focus on any.

Vata asked Pitta if she could help her plan an art show and sell the paintings to raise money for the yoga classes. Pitta was delighted to help organize and quickly began writing down ideas.

They needed to choose a name for the art show. Vata suggested that they combine the words yoga and art. Pitta replied, "YogArt, that sounds like yogurt." Vata said, "Well, I hope it's dairy free!"

Soon the art show, now named "Dairy-Free YogART", had a date, time and place! Pitta and Vata needed help telling people about the art show and needed help running the show orderly and smoothly. So they called Pitta's sister, Kapha.

Kapha was born in the cold heavy wetness of winter, and prefers warmer weather. She loves and protects her family and doesn't like to be far from home for too long. Kapha likes to move slow and can seem to be anchored down or attached to something at times. She is a good listener and will often follow the lead of her sister, Pitta. Kapha is very positive, happy and peaceful.

When Kapha notices that she has been sitting like a rock or planted like a tree for too long, she knows she needs to start flowing like water again. She likes to bring in heat and air into her yoga practice by moving fast with each breath she takes. Kapha connects to the space inside and around her by singing sounds of the universe.

Kapha came to work with Vata and Pitta to make flyers.
Then, she helped them use the computer to invite all of their
friends to the art show!

27

On the day of the art show, the Doshas were so pleased to see how their hard work had come together. They were able to work as a team. Many paintings were sold and they were able to open an organization that provides free yoga!

Just as we have the five elements inside, the Doshas can be found inside of each of us. But sometimes one or two of the Doshas will be stronger, or more dominant, than the other.

Like a fingerprint, each person is born with a unique combination of Dosha. One or two of the Dosha may be more dominant than the other. The combination of Dosha you are born with is called Prakruti.

Overtime, we grow up and life can bring on events that might switch around the combination of Dosha that we were born with. When the combination of Dosha changes, it is now called Vikruti.

Just as the Dosha sisterhood were able to work together to organize the art show, you can manage balance between the space, air, fire, water and earth elements in your own life and body.

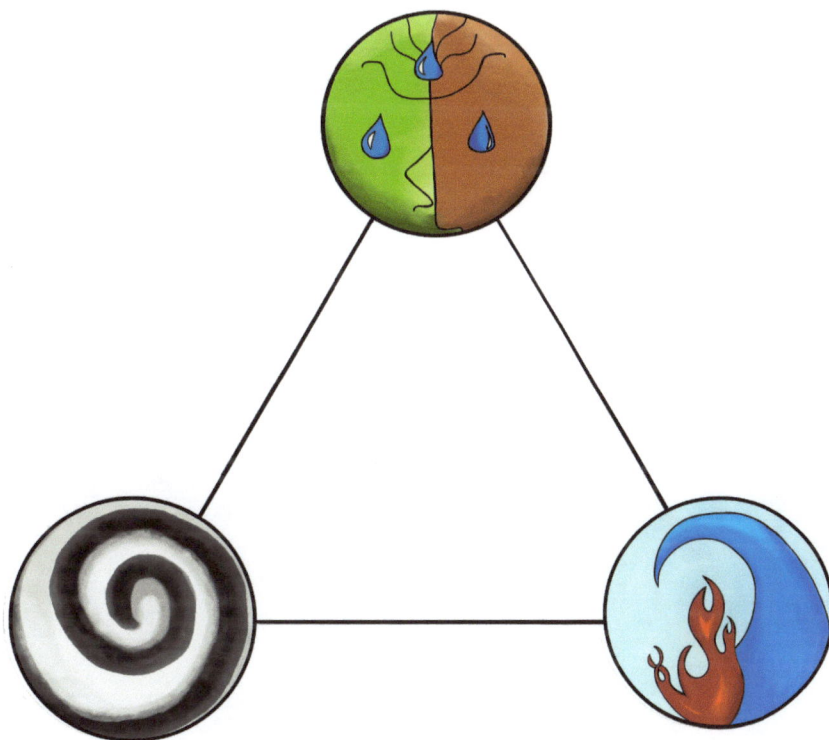

Working toward balance is always a goal in yoga. Balancing the Dosha can be accomplished through paying attention to what we eat, which is called our diet and also by meditation, calming the mind.

Namaste.

Appendix:

Suffering is created when the elements become misaligned or unbalanced in the body. For example, if you are feeling fear and worry you could have an excess of Vayu (air element) and Akasha (space element) in your body. One way to balance this is to add Jala (water element), by increasing healthy fats and oils into the diet (foods we eat), and incorporating a flowing exercise routine and practicing self-love.

Another example would be a person with an overabundance of fire could be angry or impatient and would want to avoid adding more heat. Reduce Agni (fire element), by limiting spicy foods, and adding Prithvi (earth element) by adding more protein to their diet, toning and exercising and meditating.

To learn more about the ancient practices of Yoga and Ayurveda, please consult and IAYT (International Association of Yoga Therapists) Certified Yoga Therapist or NAMA (The National Ayurvedic Medical Association) accredited Ayurvedic Practitioner.

Some of the foods that Kapha likes are:

Red Beets
Cabbage
Celery
Eggplant
Garlic
Lettuce
Mushrooms
Onions
Parsley
Peas
Radish
Spinach
Sprouts
Fennel
Brussels Sprouts
Corn
Oats
Beans
Apples
Berries
Cherries
Mangos
Peaches
Raisins
Almond Oil

Some of the foods that Vata likes are:

Asparagus
Carrots
Sweet Potatoes
Zucchini
Brown Rice
Wheat
Mung Beans
Black Lentils
Oats
Spices
Peppers
Bananas
Oranges
Peaches
Coconuts
Apples
Figs
Berries
Papayas
Pineapples
Plums
Avocados
Dried Fruit
Sesame Oil

Some of the foods that Pitta likes are:

Cabbage
Cucumber
Green Beans
Lettuce
Peas
Potatoes
Sprouts
Mushrooms
Barley
Basmati Rice
Tumeric
Cilantro
Apples
Avocados
Coconuts
Figs
Melons
Oranges
Pears
Mangos
Sunflower Oil
Coconut Oil

www.ingramcontent.com/pod-product-compliance
Lightning Source LLC
Chambersburg PA
CBHW041429090426
42741CB00003B/96